珍惜

CHERISH YOUR BODY

珍惜 Cherish Your Body

Published and translated by:
Buddhist Text Translation Society
1777 Murchison Drive
Burlingame, CA 94010-4504
www.drba.org

Printed in Taiwan

Library of Congress Cataloging-in-Publication Data

Hsuan Hua, 1908-
  Cherish your body : pearls of wisdom / by the Venerable
  Master Hua ;
  translated by Buddhist Text Translation Society.
    p. cm.
ISBN-13: 978-088139-868-7
1.   Religious life--Buddhism.   I. Buddhist Text Translation
Society. II. Title.

BQ5395.H927 2006
294.3'444--dc22
                        2005015362

獻給您——
心田有礦須開發

Dedicated to you —
The essentials to excavating the mine
in the field of the mind.

我們人有六種知覺性：
眼能見、耳能聽、鼻能嗅、
舌能嚐、身能觸、意能思想。
因為人是萬物之靈，所以具有此六種官能，
其他動物的組織就沒有那麼複雜。

我們吃飯、穿衣、睡覺，就像汽車要加油。
汽車走多了路，便要加油；
我們人把能源消耗多了，也要補充。
所以人吃飯，
就是幫助身體的新陳代謝。

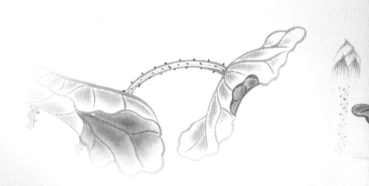

We have six perceptive faculties:
the eyes can see, the ears can hear,
the nose can smell, the tongue can taste,
the body can feel and the mind can think.

Being the most intelligent of creatures,
human beings are endowed with these
six faculties. The physical make-up
of animals is not as complex as that
of humans. We need food, clothing,
and sleep, just as a car needs gasoline to run.

After traveling many miles,
the car needs to be refueled. Likewise,
when we people have used up our energy,
we need to replenish it. That is why
we need to eat—to help sustain the
metabolism of our body.

食物在人體內發生一股熱力、一股能源，
能幫助我們一切的活動。
但實際上，食物的精華很少，
所以需要不斷地補充。

譬如早上吃了，到午間又餓；
午間吃了，到晚上又要再吃。
睡覺時也不停地消耗能源，
所以睡醒了又要吃早餐。

Food generates heat and energy
in our body, helping it to carry out
all its activities. However,
because the essence of the food that
gives us energy is actually a very small portion,
we have to constantly replenish ourselves.

For instance,
we eat breakfast in the morning,
but by noon we are hungry again;
we eat lunch, but by evening
we need to eat again.
Even when we sleep,
we are still using energy,
so when we wake up,
we are ready for breakfast again.

我們是如何消耗這個能源的？
我們的眼見色，那是在消耗能源；
耳聽聲，也是在消耗能源；
鼻聞香，也在消耗能源；
乃至舌嚐味、身覺觸、
意念在思想，
都是在消耗能源！
所以我們一舉一動、一言一行，
無不是在消耗能源。

How does our energy get used up?

When our eyes look at forms, it takes energy.

When the ears listen to sounds,

it also uses energy.

The nose smells scents,

and that uses up energy as well.

The tongue tastes flavors,

the body feels sensations,

and the mind cognizes and reflects--all

these activities exhaust our energy!

Every movement we make

and every word we say uses energy.

若你不是消耗太多，能適可而止，
身體就會保持健康；
但若是消耗太多，身體便會發生故障。
譬如：吃得太多，營養太豐富，
或者吃了有毒的東西，
這都會令身體發生毛病。

所以我們行住坐臥，一舉一動，
都要非常小心，
不要無緣無故地浪費能源，
以致傷害自己的身體及精神。
這一點是很重要的！

If we use our energy in moderation
and do not drain it completely,
our body will be healthy. If we use too much,
 our body will malfunction. For example,
if we eat too much, eat food that is too rich,
or eat something poisonous,
it will make our body sick.

So, in everything we do, whether we are
moving or still, sleeping or awake,
we should be very careful not to waste
our energy for no good reason,
or we will injure our body and mind.
This is very important.

19

小朋友！
現在是你們的黃金時代，
也是你們生命中的春天。

春天時，萬物欣欣向榮，朝氣蓬勃。

但，我們要順其自然去生長，
合乎生理的程序，
切不要亂吃亂喝，
或亂講話，或者飲酒、吃毒藥，
乃至亂看、亂聽、亂嚐、
亂嗅、亂觸、亂想，
這樣就會損害
你的身體及靈性。

Young friends! This is your golden age.
It is also the springtime of your life.

In the springtime, everything flourishes
and is full of energy. However,
we should accord with our body's
natural physical development as we grow up.

We should choose our food
and drink with care.
We should not talk recklessly,
consume alcoholic drinks, or take drugs.
We should not carelessly look at, listen to,
taste, smell, touch,
or think about improper things,
for that would hurt our body and spirit.

你會運用這六種官能，身體就健康；
不會用，身體就會隨時罷工，與你分家。
分家了！便沒得吃、沒得穿、沒有房子
睡了。

因此大家要好好愛護珍惜這個身體，
不要醉生夢死，走到極危險的歧路上。

If you know how to use
your six faculties well, you will be healthy.
If you do not, your body may go on
strike and abandon you at any time.
Then you will not be able to eat,
wear clothes, or sleep anymore.

So, all of you should take
good care of your body.
Do not live as if you are dreaming
or drunk and endanger yourself.

在《孝經》上說：
「身體髮膚，受之父母；
不敢毀傷，孝之始也。」

不要隨隨便便把自己的身體弄壞，
要好好地珍惜它，
否則便無顏見父母了。
父母生我、育我，
我們不好好珍惜身體，
那是對父母最不孝的行為。

The Classic of Filial Piety says,
"Our body, hair, and flash
are given by our parents.
Do not dare to injure them.
This is the begining of the filiality."

We should not carelessly let our body get
injured. We should cherish them with care
Otherwise,
we will not be able to face our parents.
Our parents gave birth to us and raised us;
if we fail to take care of our bodies,
we are being most unfilial to our parents.

各位善知識、教授、同學們：
今天大家有緣同聚一堂，
共同討論──
人生的需要是什麼？
我們人為什麼來到這世界上？

我們到這世界上，是不是單為吃飯、
穿衣、睡覺、享受而來的呢？
這些問題若不注意，看起來很簡單；
但若真正地去研究，
就不那麼簡單了。

All good knowing advisors, professsors,
students:

Today our affinities have brought us
together here to discuss the questions:
What are the necessities of life?
What have we come to this world for?

Have we come here solely for the purpose
of eating, wearing clothes, sleeping,
and entertaining ourselves?

These issues appear to be very simple at first,
but if we investigate them seriously,
we will find that they are not simple at all.

究竟我們人到世界來的工作是什麼？

責任是什麼？

每一個人都應認真來研討個明白。

如果認識不清楚，

此生做人就沒有什麼意義及價值。

所以我們應該認清楚如何盡責任，

如何把我們的任務做好。

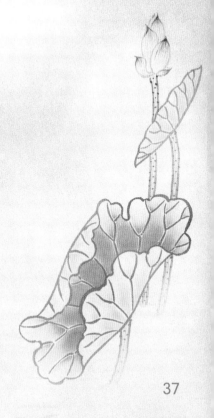

What ultimately is our work
and our responsibility for which
we have come to this world?

Each one of you should seriously look
into this until you understand it.
If you cannot figure it out,

there will not be much meaning and value
to your human existence this time around.
Therefore, we should know clearly
how we can fulfill our responsibilities
and carry out our duties well.

首先要學習
如何盡人的任務及天職。
小孩剛出世時，只會哭，只知道吃，
根本不知道他們將來的任務是什麼。
隨著時日，一天天成長，
父母就送他們到學校
去學習做人的責任，
以準備將來盡自己的任務。

41

First of all, we must learn how to fulfill
our natural human duties and obligations.
Newborn babies know only how to cry
and drink milk.
They have no idea of what
their future responsibilities will be.

As the days go by and they gradually grow up,
their parents will send them to school
to learn the basic human obligations so that
they can fulfill their roles in the future.

學習的時候，每個人有種種志願。
有的是為學「明理」，明白道理；
有的為了「名利」，
將來好出風頭，得個好名譽；

有的為將來能發財，得大利益，
根本不管明不明理、合不合法，
不擇手段去發財、爭取權利。

Everyone has different resolve
in terms of study.
Some study in order to "understand principle"
(Chinese: 明理 mingli);
while others study for the purpose of obtaining
"fame and profit"
(also mingli, but the characters are different).

Some study because they want to have a
big fortune and to gain large profits.
They do not care whether
they understand principle,
or if what they do is legal.
They want to get rich any way they can,
and they are out for power.

有的人有「領袖欲」，要作領導者。
但，這你先要知道如何做人，
看自己是否夠得上做一個人的資格。
如果明白如何做人，能做別人的模範，
那你做領袖是於心無愧的。
若心存爭心、貪心、求心、
自私心、自利心、打妄語心，
向外馳求，做領袖只為自己謀福利，
而不能為他人謀幸福，那就是走錯路了。

做領袖，一定要屈己待人，
薄己厚人，利益所有人類。

Some have the desire for leadership:
they want to be leaders.
But they should first of all know
how to be people.
Do they meet the standards
of human conduct?
If you understand how to be a person
and can act as a model for others,
then you can confidently assume
a leadership role.
If you have thoughts of contention, greed,
seeking, selfishness, wanting personal profit,
or lying; if you seek things outside; and,
if you want to be a leader in order to
benefit yourself and not others,
then you are going down the wrong road.
As a leader, you must humble
yourself to serve others,
be hard on yourself and good to others,
and benefit all humankind.

做人的責任是什麼呢？
就是應該對全世界有所貢獻，有所幫助。
利益世界上所有的人，
是我們每個人做人真正的責任；
而不是專為自己能吃一點好的，
穿一點好的，住一間豪華的房子而已。

What are our responsibilities as human beings?
We should make some contribution
to help the whole world and benefit
all the people of the world.

This is every person's true responsibility.
We are not here merely to eat good food,
wear nice clothes,
or live in a luxurious house.

應該是：
普天下，
若有一人沒有飯吃、沒有衣穿，
那是我對不起這個人；
因為我沒有盡到
自己的心力來幫助他。

所以，做人真正的責任，
就是要真正利益他人；
要有功於世，有利於民，
這是我應負起的責任，不可推諉。
人人都存這種心，
世界一定和平沒有戰爭。

If there is one person on earth who does
not have food to eat and clothes to wear,
then I have failed that person,
because I have not tried my best and
applied all my effort to help him or her.

Our real duty as human beings is
to truly benefit others;
we must make a contribution to the world
and benefit the people.
We should take this duty upon ourselves
and not shift it to others.
If everyone can think like this,
the world will surely be peaceful
and free of wars.

首先，
我們要做人的好模範，不與人爭。
世界為什麼壞？
就因為爭權、爭利、爭名。

如果你能將好事讓給他人，
旁人不願意的事，你願意接受過來，
和所有人都不爭；
像這樣——人人都不爭，
世界和平一定有望。

First of all, we should be good models
for others by not contending with people.
Why is this world so chaotic?
Because people fight for power,
profit, and fame.

You should yield the good things to others,
and take the things that no one else wants;
do not contend with people.
If everyone can refrain from contention,
there is certainly hope for world peace.

一般人所貪的，你不貪，
不隨世界瘋狂的風氣跑，
而作疾風中的勁燭，烈火中的精金，

隨緣不變，不變隨緣，
抱定自己的宗旨，潛移默化，
令人人遵守不爭、不貪、不求、
不自私、不自利、不妄語，
那麼世界一定和平。

65

Do not covet the things that ordinary
people are greedy for.
Do not go along with the foolish
trends of the world.
Be a sturdy candle that cannot be
blown out by a fierce wind.

Be like a lump of pure gold in a blazing fire.
Adapt to conditions but never change;
remain steadfast while according
with every condition;
hold to your own principles; and,
silently influence people to observe
the principles of no fighting, no greed,
no seeking, no selfishness,
no pursuit of personal advantage,
and no lying. If you can do all this,
the world will certainly be peaceful.

從自己修身起，
在內心與自己不爭，
則一切發狂妄想都不起了，
平平靜靜，這就是真正的快樂。

你自己平靜快樂，
就能影響旁人都平靜快樂。
大家和平相處，
世界就不會有戰爭。

Begin by cultivating yourself.
When you do not fight with yourself in your
own mind, foolish false thoughts will cease
to arise and you will feel very peaceful.
That is true happiness.

When you are peaceful and happy,
you will influence the people around
you to feel peaceful and happy, too.
When everyone lives in harmony,
the world will no longer have wars.

為什麼世界有戰爭？
就因為人在心裏爭的緣故。
人心和平，
則世界和平；
人心不平，
則世界不和平。

我們青年人、老年人
認識這個道理後，
就不會賭博、吸毒、
放火、搶劫、強姦。

Why are there wars in the world?
Because people fight in their minds.
If people's minds are at peace,
the world will be at peace.
If people's minds are not peaceful,
then the world will not be peaceful.

When all of us, young and old,
truly understand this principle,
we will no longer go gambling,
take drugs, set fires, rob or rape.

要想世界好，先要從自己做起。
若我不好，世界怎麼會好呢？

不要專指著他人說：
「為什麼別人不守規矩？」
你要先問自己「守規矩沒有？」

青年人要負起這個責任來，
青年人不好好做，
世界怎麼會好？

If we want this world to be good,
we have to start with ourselves. If I am not good,
how can I expect the world be good?

We should not always point to others and say,
"Why don't they follow the rules?"
You should first ask yourself
"Have I followed the rules?"

Young people should take up this responsibility.
If young people do not behave well,
how can the world turn out well?

青年人從教授和老師那兒——
學往正道走。
但，若找到不好的老師，
教他們邪知邪見，
青年人也跟著學壞。
所謂：
「近朱者赤，近墨者黑」；
因此，擇友尋師是非常重要的。

Young people learn from their teachers
and professors to walk the right path.
However, if they have bad teachers who
teach them deviant views and knowledge,
they will likewise turn out bad.

As it is said,
"One who draws near crimson becomes red;
one who draws near ink becomes black."
Therefore, selecting friends and seeking
teachers are very important matters.

有為的青年
應將自己責任認識清楚，
不要作個自了漢。
做人的責任是要有功於世，
有益於民，有利於全人類。

我本來想要負起救世的責任，
成就全世界人類；
但我老了，力量不夠，
所以我寄望各位有為的青年，
要發起救世的心，
為全人類謀幸福。

Capable young people should
clearly recognize their own responsibilities
and not be selfish individuals who only
look out for themselves.
Our human duty is to make contributions
to the world, help people,
and benefit all of humankind.

Originally, I wanted to take up
the responsibility of saving the world, and help
all humankind to realize great achievements.
But I am getting old and do not have enough
strength. Thus, I am hoping that all of you
capable young people will resolve to save
the world and seek blessings for humankind.

有為的青年們！
應該真正發大願大力，
來成就全世界人類的幸福，
拯救那些處在水深火熱的人，
令他們離苦得樂。

首先，自己要先學不抽菸、
不喝酒、不發脾氣、不殺生、
不偷盜、不邪婬、不妄語、
不吃肉、不賭博、不吸毒，
要學正當的行為，
這樣全世界人類才會得救。

All of you capable young people!
You should sincerely make great vows
and bring forth great strength to help all
of humankind achieve happiness.

You should help those caught in deep
waters and burning fires to leave suffering
and find happiness.

First of all, you should learn not to smoke,
not to drink, not to lose your temper,
not to kill, not to steal,
not to engage in sexual misconduct,
not to lie, not to eat meat, not to gamble,
and not to take drugs. You should learn to
conduct yourselves properly.
If you can be like this, then the people
of the world will eventually be saved.

我到處大聲疾呼，
希望年輕人覺悟，
發大慈大悲、大喜大捨的心，
秉著像耶穌、釋迦牟尼佛，
及所有聖人的救世胸懷，
那麼世界即使不和平，也要和平了。
今天所講的，各位可以研究研究；
講的對不對？我不知道。

我是一個極渴望世界和平的人，
希望世界人類沒有痛苦，
但完成這個理想，
一定要有智慧才能做到的。

Everywhere I go,
I call on the young people to bring
forth hearts of great kindness,
great compassion, great joy, and
great renunciation, and to emulate the resolve
that Jesus Christ, Shakyamuni Buddha,
and all other sages have to save the world.
Then it would be impossible
for peace not to prevail.

All of you can look into what I said today.
I do not know if what I said is right.

I am a person who longs for world peace
and hopes the people of the world
will be free from suffering. However,
it will take wisdom to realize this ideal.

法界佛教總會簡介

法界佛教總會——簡稱「法總」

· 創辦人——宣化上人。

· 以法界為體，將佛教的真實義理，傳播到世界各地為目的；以翻譯經典、弘揚正法、提倡道德教育、利樂一切有情為己任。

· 以不爭、不貪、不求、不自私、不自利、不妄語為宗旨。

· 有萬佛聖城等近三十座道場，遍佈美、亞洲；其僧眾均須恪遵佛制：日中一食、衣不離體，持戒念佛，習教參禪，和合共住，獻身佛教。

· 有國際譯經學院、法界宗教研究院、僧伽居士訓練班、法界佛教大學、培德中學、育良小學等機構。

· 本會道場、機構，門戶開放，凡各國各教人士，願致力於仁義道德、明心見性者，歡迎前來共同研習！

DRBA

An Introduction to the Dharma Realm Buddhist Association (DRBA)

- Founder: Venerable Master Hsuan Hua
- Taking the Dharma Realm as its substance, DRBA seeks to disseminate the true principles of Buddhism to all areas of the world. Its missions are to translate the Buddhist scriptures, to propagate the orthodox Dharma, to promote ethics-based education, and to benefit all sentient beings.
- The guiding principles of DRBA are: no contention, no greed, no seeking, no selfishness, no seeking of personal advantage, and no lying.
- In addition to the City of Ten Thousand Buddhas, DRBA has nearly thirty branch monasteries located throughout the United States, Canada and Asia. DRBA'S Sangha members honor the rules and practices

established by the Buddha: eating only one meal a day, always wearing the precept sash, observing the precepts and being mindful of the Buddha, studying the Buddha's teachings, practicing meditation, living together in harmony, and dedicating their lives to Buddhism.

- DRBA'S institutions include the International Institute for the Translation of Buddhist Texts, the Institute for World Religions, the Sangha and Laity Training Programs, Dharma Realm Buddhist University, Developing Virtue Secondary School, and Instilling Goodness Elementary School.

- The doors of DRBA's monasteries and institutions are open to anyone from any country who wishes to devote themselves to the pursuit of humaneness, justice, and ethics, and the discovery of their true mind.

宣化上人簡傳

來自白雪皚皚的中國東北──長白山區。

十九歲出家修道，發願普渡一切衆生。

一九六二年將正確真實的佛法，

由東方帶到西方──美國。

一九六八年五位美國人在上人座下出家，

是在西方建立三寶的第一人。

「美國法界佛教總會」創辦人，

分支道場遍佈美、加、亞、澳地區。

建立美國第一座佛教大道場──萬佛聖城。

一九九五年圓寂，「我從虛空來，回到虛空去」。

終其一生儘量幫助世界走向安樂光明的途徑，

大慈悲普渡，流血汗，不休息！

A Brief Introduction to
the Venerable Master Hsuan Hua

He came from the snow-laden country near the Eternally White Mountains in northeastern China.

At the age of nineteen, he became a Buddhist monk and vowed to save all living beings.

In 1962, he brought the Proper Buddhadharma from East to West (i.e., the U.S.).

In 1968, five Americans took monastic vows under his guidance. Thus, he was the first person to establish the Triple Jewel on American soil.

He founded the Dharma Realm Buddhist Association, with branch monasteries in the United States, Canada, Asia and Australia.

He established the City of Ten Thousand Buddhas, the first large Buddhist monastic community in America

In 1995, before he passed into stillness, he said, "I came from empty space, and to empty space I will return."

Throughout his life, through his own sweat and blood, he helped the world walk towards the path of peace and light, compassionately and tirelessly rescuing living beings.

法界佛教總會・萬佛聖城
Dharma Realm Buddhist Association &
The City of Ten Thousand Buddhas
4951 Bodhi Way, Ukiah, CA 95482 USA
Tel: (707) 462-0939   Fax: (707) 462-0949
http://www.drba.org , www.drbachinese.org

國際譯經學院 The International Translation Institute
1777 Murchison Drive, Burlingame, CA 94010-4504 U.S.A.
Tel: (650) 692-5912   Fax: (650) 692-5056

法界宗教研究院（柏克萊寺）
Institute for World Religions(at Berkeley Buddhist Monastery)
2304 McKinley Avenue, Berkeley, CA 94703 U.S.A.
Tel: (510) 848-3440   Fax: (510) 548-4551

金山聖寺 Gold Mountain Monastery
800 Sacramento Street, San Francisco, CA 94108 U.S.A.
Tel: (415) 421-6117   Fax: (415) 788-6001

金聖寺 Gold Sage Monastery
11455 Clayton Road, San Jose, CA 95127 U.S.A.
Tel: (408) 923-7243   Fax: (408) 923-1064

法界聖城 City of the Dharma Realm
1029 West Capitol Avenue, West Sacramento, CA 95691 U.S.A.
Tel/Fax: (916) 374-8268

金輪聖寺 Gold Wheel Monastery
235 North Avenue 58, Los Angeles, CA 90042 U.S.A.
Tel/Fax: (323) 258-6668

長堤聖寺 Long Beach Monastery
3361 East Ocean Boulevard, Long Beach, CA 90803 U.S.A.
Tel/Fax: (562) 438-8902

華嚴精舍 Avatamsaka Hermitage
9601 Seven Locks Road, Bethesda, MD 20817-9997 USA
Tel/Fax: (301) 469-8300

金峰聖寺 Gold Summit Monastery
233 First Avenue West, Seattle, WA 98119 U.S.A.
Tel: (206) 284-6690   Fax: (206) 284-6918

金佛聖寺 **Gold Buddha Monastery**
248 E. 11th Avenue, Vancouver, B.C. V5T 2C3 Canada
Tel: (604) 709-0248   Fax: (604) 684-3754

華嚴聖寺 **Avatamsaka Monastery**
1009 Fourth Avenue S.W., Calgary, AB T2P 0K8 Canada
Tel/Fax: (403) 234-0644

金岸法界 **Gold Coast Dharma Realm**
106 Bonogin Road, Mudgeeraba, QLD. 4213 Australia
Tel: (07) 5522-8788; 5520-1188

法界佛教印經會 **Dharma Realm Buddhist Books Distribution Society**
臺灣省臺北市忠孝東路六段 85 號 11 樓
Tel: (02) 2786-3022, 2786-2474   Fax: (02) 2786-2674

法界聖寺 **Dharma Realm Monastery**
臺灣省高雄縣六龜鄉興龍村東溪山莊 20 號
Tel: (07) 689-3713   Fax: (07) 689-3870

彌陀聖寺 **Amitabha Monastery**
臺灣省花蓮縣壽豐鄉池南村四健會 7 號   Tel: (03) 865-1956   Fax: (03) 865-3426

佛教講堂 **Buddhist Lecture Hall**
香港跑馬地黃泥涌道 31 號 11 樓
31 Wong Nei Chong Road, Top Floor, Happy Valley, Hong Kong, China
Tel: 2572-7644   Fax: 2572-2850

般若觀音聖寺 (紫雲洞)
Prajna Guan Yin Sagely Monastery (Formerly Tze Yun Tung Temple)
Batu 5 1/2, Jalan Sungai Besi, Salak Selatan,
57100 Kuala Lumpur, West Malaysia   Tel: (03)7982-6560 Fax: (03)7980-1272

法界觀音聖寺 (登彼岸)
Dharma Realm Guanyin Sagely Monastery (Formerly Deng Bi An Temple)
161, Jalan Ampang, 50450 Kuala Lumpur, Malaysia
Tel: (03) 2164-8055 Fax: (03) 2163-7118

馬來西亞法界佛教總會檳城分會
Malaysia Dharma Realm Buddhist Association Penang Branch
32-32C, Jalan Tan Sri Teh Ewe Lim,
11600 Jelutong,Penang, Malaysia
Tel: (04)281-7728 Fax: (04)281-7798

CHERISH YOUR BODY

作　者　宣化上人
插畫者　鍾美雨

發行人　法界佛教總會
出　版　法界佛教總會・佛經翻譯委員會・法界佛教大學
　　　　The City of Ten Thousand Buddhas(萬佛聖城)
地　址　4951 Bodhi Way, Ukiah, CA 95482 USA
　　　　Tel: (707) 462-0939　Fax: (707)462-0949
　　　　http://www.drba.org , www.drbachinese.org

　　　　The International Translation Institute
　　　　1777 Murchison Drive Burlingame,
　　　　CA 94010-4504 U.S.A.
　　　　Tel: (650) 692-5912　Fax: (650) 692-5056

倡　印　萬佛聖城　The City of Ten Thousand Buddhas

　　　　法界佛教印經會
　　　　臺灣省臺北市忠孝東路六段 85 號 11 樓
　　　　電話: (02) 2786-3022, 2786-2474
　　　　www.drbataipei.org

出版日　2007 年 5 月 2 日・初版二刷
ISBN 978-088139-868-7